FRANCIS FRITH'S

PENRITH

PHOTOGRAPHIC MEMORIES

A Northumbrian with Eden ancestors, **DR SYDNEY CHAPMAN** gained Honours in Latin and Greek and a PhD at Durham; an MPhil in Art Gallery and Museum Studies from Manchester followed for research on Lake District heritage. He is an Honorary Visiting Fellow at Lancaster University.

JUDITH CLARKE was born and educated in Cumbria. She began her museum career at Carlisle's Tullie House Museum and Art Gallery in 1970 where for a period of ten years she was responsible for its Decorative Arts collections. She holds a post-graduate Diploma from the Museums Association and a Masters Degree in Museum and Heritage Management.

The authors jointly curate Penrith Museum.

FRANCIS FRITH'S
PHOTOGRAPHIC MEMORIES

PENRITH

PHOTOGRAPHIC MEMORIES

DR SYDNEY T CHAPMAN
& JUDITH CLARKE

First published in the United Kingdom in 2005 by
The Francis Frith Collection®

Hardback edition published in 2005 ISBN 1-84589-019-1

Paperback edition 2005 ISBN 1-85937-968-0

British Library Cataloguing in Publication Data

Penrith - Photographic Memories
Dr Sydney T Chapman & Judith Clarke

The Francis Frith Collection
Frith's Barn, Teffont,
Salisbury, Wiltshire SP3 5QP
Tel: +44 (0) 1722 716 376
Email: info@francisfrith.co.uk
www.francisfrith.co.uk

Printed and bound in Great Britain

Front Cover: **PENRITH**, *Cornmarket c1955* P33013t
Frontispiece: **PENRITH**, *Devonshire Street c1955* P33024

*The colour-tinting is for illustrative purposes only, and is not intended
to be historically accurate*

Aerial photographs reproduced under licence from
Simmons Aerofilms Limited.
Historical Ordnance Survey maps reproduced under licence from
Homecheck.co.uk
Every attempt has been made to contact copyright holders of
illustrative material. We will be happy to give full acknowledgement
in future editions for any items not credited. Any information
should be directed to The Francis Frith Collection.

AS WITH ANY HISTORICAL DATABASE THE FRITH ARCHIVE IS
CONSTANTLY BEING CORRECTED AND IMPROVED AND THE
PUBLISHERS WOULD WELCOME INFORMATION ON OMISSIONS OR
INACCURACIES

CONTENTS

FRANCIS FRITH: VICTORIAN PIONEER   7

PENRITH - AN INTRODUCTION   10

AROUND PENRITH   15

PENRITH FROM THE AIR   34

PENRITH FROM THE AIR   36

NORTH TO NUNNERY WALKS   38

ORDNANCE SURVEY MAP   48

EAST TO MORLAND   50

COUNTY MAP   62

SOUTH TO HAWESWATER   64

WEST TO GREYSTOKE AND ULLSWATER   78

INDEX   87

NAMES OF PRE-PUBLICATION BUYERS   88

Free Mounted Print Voucher   91

FRANCIS FRITH
VICTORIAN PIONEER

FRANCIS FRITH, founder of the world-famous photographic archive, was a complex and multi-talented man. A devout Quaker and a highly successful Victorian businessman, he was philosophical by nature and pioneering in outlook.

By 1855 he had already established a wholesale grocery business in Liverpool, and sold it for the astonishing sum of £200,000, which is the equivalent today of over £15,000,000. Now a very rich man, he was able to indulge his passion for travel. As a child he had pored over travel books written by early explorers, and his fancy and imagination had been stirred by family holidays to the sublime mountain regions of Wales and Scotland. 'What lands of spirit-stirring and enriching scenes and places!' he had written. He was to return to these scenes of grandeur in later years to 'recapture the thousands of vivid and tender memories', but with a different purpose. Now in his thirties, and captivated by the new science of photography, Frith set out on a series of pioneering journeys up the Nile and to the Near East that occupied him from 1856 until 1860.

INTRIGUE AND EXPLORATION

These far-flung journeys were packed with intrigue and adventure. In his life story, written when he was sixty-three, Frith tells of being held captive by bandits, and of fighting 'an awful midnight battle to the very point of surrender with a deadly pack of hungry, wild dogs'. Wearing flowing Arab costume, Frith arrived at Akaba by camel sixty years before Lawrence of Arabia, where he encountered 'desert princes and rival sheikhs, blazing with jewel-hilted swords'.

He was the first photographer to venture beyond the sixth cataract of the Nile. Africa was still the mysterious 'Dark Continent', and Stanley and Livingstone's historic meeting was a decade into the future. The conditions for picture taking confound belief. He laboured for hours in his wicker dark-room in the sweltering heat of the desert, while the volatile chemicals fizzed dangerously in their trays. Back in London he exhibited his photographs and was 'rapturously cheered' by members of the Royal Society. His reputation as a photographer was made overnight.

VENTURE OF A LIFE-TIME

Characteristically, Frith quickly spotted the opportunity to create a new business as a specialist publisher of photographs. He lived in an era of immense and sometimes violent change.

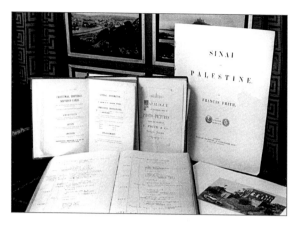

For the poor in the early part of Victoria's reign work was exhausting and the hours long, and people had precious little free time to enjoy themselves. Most had no transport other than a cart or gig at their disposal, and rarely travelled far beyond the boundaries of their own town or village. However, by the 1870s the railways had threaded their way across the country, and Bank Holidays and half-day Saturdays had been made obligatory by Act of Parliament. All of a sudden the working man and his family were able to enjoy days out and see a little more of the world.

With typical business acumen, Francis Frith foresaw that these new tourists would enjoy having souvenirs to commemorate their days out. In 1860 he married Mary Ann Rosling and set out on a new career: his aim was to photograph every city, town and village in Britain. For the next thirty years he travelled the country by train and by pony and trap, producing fine photographs of seaside resorts and beauty spots that were keenly bought by millions of Victorians. These prints were painstakingly pasted into family albums and pored over during the dark nights of winter, rekindling precious memories of summer excursions.

THE RISE OF FRITH & CO

Frith's studio was soon supplying retail shops all over the country. To meet the demand he gathered about him a small team of photographers, and published the work of independent artist-photographers of the calibre of Roger Fenton and Francis Bedford. In order to gain some understanding of the scale of Frith's business one only has to look at the catalogue issued by Frith & Co in 1886: it runs to some 670 pages, listing not only many thousands of views of the British Isles but also many photographs of most European countries, and China, Japan, the USA and Canada - note the sample page shown on page 9 from the hand-written Frith & Co ledgers recording the pictures. By 1890 Frith had created the greatest specialist photographic publishing company in the world, with over 2,000 sales outlets - more than the combined number that Boots and WH Smith have today! The picture on the next page shows the Frith & Co display board at Ingleton in the Yorkshire Dales (left of window). Beautifully constructed with a mahogany frame and gilt inserts, it could display up to a dozen local scenes.

POSTCARD BONANZA

The ever-popular holiday postcard we know today took many years to develop. In 1870 the Post Office issued the first plain cards, with a pre-printed stamp on one face. In 1894 they allowed other publishers' cards to be sent through the mail with an attached adhesive halfpenny stamp. Demand grew rapidly, and in 1895 a new size of postcard was permitted called the court card, but there was little room for illustration. In 1899, a year after Frith's death, a new card measuring 5.5 x 3.5 inches became the standard format, but it was not until 1902 that the divided back came into being, so that the address and message could be on one face and a full-size illustration on the other. Frith & Co were in the vanguard of postcard development: Frith's sons Eustace and Cyril continued their father's monumental task, expanding the number of views offered to the public and recording more and more places

in Britain, as the coasts and countryside were opened up to mass travel.

Francis Frith had died in 1898 at his villa in Cannes, his great project still growing. The archive he created continued in business for another seventy years. By 1970 it contained over a third of a million pictures showing 7,000 British towns and villages.

FRANCIS FRITH'S LEGACY

Frith's legacy to us today is of immense significance and value, for the magnificent archive of evocative photographs he created provides a unique record of change in the cities, towns and villages throughout Britain over a century and more. Frith and his fellow studio photographers revisited locations many times down the years to update their views, compiling for us an enthralling and colourful pageant of British life and character.

We are fortunate that Frith was dedicated to recording the minutiae of everyday life, for it is this sheer wealth of visual data, the painstaking chronicle of changes in dress, transport, street layouts, buildings, housing, engineering and landscape that captivates us so much today. His remarkable images offer us a powerful link with the past and with the lives of our ancestors.

THE VALUE OF THE ARCHIVE TODAY

Computers have now made it possible for Frith's many thousands of images to be accessed almost instantly. Frith's images are increasingly used as visual resources, by social historians, by researchers into genealogy and ancestry, by architects and town planners, and by teachers involved in local history projects.

In addition, the archive offers every one of us an opportunity to examine the places where we and our families have lived and worked down the years. Highly successful in Frith's own era, the archive is now, a century and more on, entering a new phase of popularity. Historians consider the Francis Frith Collection to be of prime national importance. It is the only archive of its kind remaining in private ownership. Francis Frith's archive is now housed in an historic timber barn in the beautiful village of Teffont in Wiltshire. Its founder would not recognize the archive office as it is today. In place of the many thousands of dusty boxes containing glass plate negatives and an all-pervading odour of photographic chemicals, there are now ranks of computer screens. He would be amazed to watch his images travelling round the world at unimaginable speeds through internet lines.

The archive's future is both bright and exciting. Francis Frith, with his unshakeable belief in making photographs available to the greatest number of people, would undoubtedly approve of what is being done today with his lifetime's work. His photographs depicting our shared past are now bringing pleasure and enlightenment to millions around the world a century and more after his death.

PENRITH
AN INTRODUCTION

WHILE the photographs in this book are centred on the historic market town of Penrith, also included are views of some of the villages in the Eden Valley and on the northern edge of the Lake District which surround it.

Penrith is the administrative centre for the Eden District of Cumbria, an extensive predominantly rural area containing within its boundaries large tracts of the Lake District National Park, the Pennines and the Howgill Fells; these encircle the valley through which flow rivers which include the Eden, Lowther, and the Eamont, all of which spring from their slopes.

There is some uncertainty as to the origin of the name 'Penrith', which some say is derived from the town's situation under the 'red hill'. Alternatively the name could have described its position as the 'chief ford', although the ford in question would have been the crossing point on the River Eamont about a mile south. In the early 10th century the river probably demarcated England from Scotland, being the southernmost frontier of the semi-independent British Kingdom of Strathclyde. For centuries the same river would be the boundary between the former counties of Cumberland and Westmorland which, together with Lancashire north of the Sands, were united to form the greater county of Cumbria in 1974.

From its source in Mallerstang Common the River Eden flows for the greater part of its course almost due north, passing through gently undulating country which shows the smoothing effects of the northward passage of a powerful valley glacier. The Eden Valley's geology of soft Permian and Triassic sandstones, mudstones and shales has shaped its landscape and life. The red sandstones which give the area much of its character outcrop as a series of hills between the Rivers Eden and Petteril north of Penrith, and form distinctive gorges where the River Eden has cut down through the rock north of Kirkoswald and at Armathwaite.

The Eden Valley's gently sloping topography contrasts with the steep, 'harder' ground of the Pennine escarpment flanking it, and the limestone country around the Orton and Asby Fells and eastern slopes of the Lake District. The proximity of these wilder 'fells' constantly inclines one to appreciate more acutely the richness and sheltered aspect of the terrain lying below them. It is a largely agricultural landscape with scattered farms loosely based around villages. One is never far from belts of ancient, semi-natural woodland, large coniferous or broad-leaved plantations or small copses and pockets of mire and rough grassland - all havens for a variety of wildlife. The river system is especially interesting, being home to species of European importance.

The valley was one of the major folk routes of prehistoric times, to the south crossing the Pennines via Stainmore leading to the Vale of York, and to the north reaching through the Irthing Valley to the Tyne Gap. It was, however, not merely a thoroughfare; there were considerable inducements to attract settlers. The river provided fresh water, food and a means of transport, while the sandstone tracts with their thin cover of lighter soils offered dry habitation sites in a relatively sheltered area. There is evidence of widespread settlement from prehistoric times in the form of large stone circles and ritual burials, with a general scatter of contemporary artefacts. These indicate the surprising level of organisation the early inhabitants attained. Since then humans have occupied virtually every part of the valley exploiting its resources of game, timber, minerals and stone. They have tended herds or shepherded flocks grazing its pastures and slopes and farmed fertile soil.

Advances in manufacturing and technology from Roman and medieval times onwards have combined with population growth to change the landscape. One notable check to such development was the creation of the Forest of Inglewood, a hunting reserve held by the

Norman kings where wild animals such as boar and deer were afforded some protection and extensive areas of woodland were planted and managed for economic reasons. From the 18th century onwards, the owners of large estates developed their parklands, laid out their gardens or improved and farmed land that had been 'enclosed'.

Penrith appears to have been a township with sufficient municipal importance to merit its own official seal. In the 1830s the original 14th-century brass seal was discovered in a ditch beside the old church at Brampton, some twenty miles to the north east – dropped, it is thought, by Scots raiders following one of their forays in the area. This relic came into the possession of Mr R Ferguson, MP for Carlisle, who gave it to the old Penrith Local Board of Health in 1876. Bearing the cross of St Andrew and the inscription 'Sigillum Commune Ville de Penreth' (The Common Seal of the Town of Penrith) its design was subsequently adopted as the insignia of the Penrith Urban District Council in 1894. It is now on display in Penrith Museum.

Penrith is still the important focus for trade and commerce that it was even in the early medieval period. As early as 1223, Henry III had granted the town the right to hold a market every Wednesday and allowed timber to be taken from Inglewood Forest for the building of shops and stalls. Newcomers to the town were allowed ten oak trees each to build on rented sites. The first market site was probably in Burrowgate which, with Sandgate, are thought to be the oldest streets in Penrith. In 1789, James Clarke's 'Survey of the Lakes of Cumberland, Westmorland and Lancashire' described the markets as 'disposed in a manner truly astonishing in so small a town; the wheat market is in one part, the rye and potatoes in another, barley in another, oats and peas in another; live cattle, horses and hogs all have their distinct markets'. By this date we find that market day had been altered from Wednesday to Tuesday, and Saturday was also a market day.

A considerable amount of Penrith's trade and commerce was generated by the markets. There was a weekly corn market, fortnightly cattle and sheep markets, special great fairs for horses, cattle and other livestock, and servants' hiring fairs at Martinmas and Whitsun.

The market stalls and pitches were rented. Tolls were taken 'for the making cleane of the streets', and the office of 'metlaw and weighlaw' received as its dues 'a dish full of corn and salte that cometh to be sold in the market of Penrith, and of every woolsacke 4d.' In 1855 disputes arose about the size of the multure dishes used to take the tolls. New dishes were agreed upon holding a quart for oats, and six and three quarters and three gills for wheat, rye and barley. In 1878 the Penrith Local Board of Health bought the markets for £4,140, having previously leased them from the Duke of Devonshire. Two years later the tolls were altered to payments of money but the old brass and wood multure dishes used to collect the tolls by the Board of Health have survived and can be seen in the town's museum.

In the early years of the 19th century the area around the market place in the centre of Penrith was much busier and more crowded with buildings than it is today. There still stood the Old Moot Hall, the Cross and Proclamation Stone, the Shambles, as well as a large building known as the Roundabout. All, apart from the Roundabout, had disappeared by 1809, but the latter did not last much longer, being sold by public auction in May 1826, and demolished soon after.

The public houses, taverns and inns of the town thrived on the trade generated by the

PENRITH, *Askham Bridge 1893* 32945

people who flocked to the markets. In addition to all this bustle, Scottish drovers led their cattle through Penrith's great thoroughfare on their long southward journey to the capital. The inns served long-distance travellers crossing the unrelenting and bleak Shap fell journeying between Kendal and Carlisle, some with more distant destinations like London or Scotland; others traversed the exposed heights of Stainmore to Durham and the vale of York.

In 1829 there were 58 establishments serving drink and providing accommodation, giving employment to a great number of people, including ostlers and grooms for the horses. The horse and carriage business was hit by the arrival of rail travel. In 1838 the extension of the railway through eastern England into Scotland was completed, making unnecessary the westward coach journey to Scotland from Scotch Corner via Penrith and Carlisle. Soon after, in 1846, the London to Carlisle railway was eventually extended from Lancaster to Penrith and Carlisle. Even so the horse-drawn carrier trade thrived continuously throughout the century, taking produce and passengers to these rail-heads. With repairs to carriages and coaches and general agricultural improvements the blacksmithing trade grew. Altham's foundry was in business by 1831 and Stalker's Foundry was set up in Castlegate by the mid 1850s. The latter was renowned for its prize ploughs, some of them of innovative design.

The building of the railway through Penrith had occasioned one of the most tense moments in its history, when the 'Navvy Riot' threatened to turn the town into a field of battle between opposing gangs of English and Irish workmen who had long been at loggerheads. The Westmorland and Cumberland Yeomanry, the region's volunteer militia, staged a magnificent show of strength and - with the help of the local padre who pleaded with the Irishmen - pacified the town without any loss of life or serious injury being inflicted.

By the end of the 18th century Penrith had acquired a considerable reputation for the

PENRITH, *Lowther Castle 1894* 33514

manufacture of 'checks' for aprons and bed hangings, linen cloth for shirting and sheeting and for ginghams. By the 1830s production was centred on factories in Carlisle though, remarkably, Morland village could boast one factory which processed flax which was sent out to be spun and woven by cottagers in their own homes. Another home industry in the Eden Valley was the knitting of gloves and socks, much of it destined for armies at home and abroad. The decoratively carved wooden knitting sticks which were once frequently encountered in antique shops are a reminder of the days when the volume of such work led to the development of these artefacts. Their purpose was in fact to maximise efficiency by making the routine less tiring to the arms. Again examples can be seen in Penrith's museum. The tanning trade was also important to Penrith, tanneries or barkhouses being mentioned in deeds from 1379 to the 1550s. This in turn supported the allied occupations of saddlers, cobblers, shoemakers and glovers.

With an economy driven by manual work and long distance travel the fact that Penrith once had several notable breweries needs little explanation. The Old Brewery in Stricklandgate, established in 1754, was eventually purchased by Glasson's Brewery whose own premises were a former tannery in Union Court, off Roper Street. At various times there were also breweries in Middlegate, Burrowgate and Great Dockray.

The following photographs range over an area which is never far from the sight of Penrith's famous Beacon, a monument looking down on landscapes and scenes all of which have their own particular interest, attraction or place in history. It is with the aim of showing how this selection of fleeting images from the past brings these into focus that we now tour the district with our commentary.

AROUND
PENRITH

PENRITH, *The View from
the Beacon towards Ullswater 1893* 32930

Though the M6 now traces a line across the middle ground, a walk
up Beacon Fell is still rewarded by this panorama over to the Lake
District. The view was enjoyed by Wordsworth, whose mother and
her parents were Penrithians, and whose father came from nearby
Sockbridge. The Fell and the historical and scenic attractions
below it are described in Wordsworth's verse, a reminder that he is
not exclusively the poet of the landscape on the horizon.

PENRITH
The Beacon c1955
P33011

Built in 1719 on the site of earlier fire-signal stations, the Beacon stands almost 1,000ft above sea-level, commanding views of the Lakeland, Pennine and Shap Fells and Scottish mountains. Its flames flashed warnings during the Napoleonic wars and second Jacobite Rebellion.

PENRITH, *Aerial View c1953* P33019

Here a warren of properties north-west of the church is seen reaching into Burrowgate, the probable site of the early town or 'burgh'. It skirts Sandgate where a coach faces ancient dwellings in front of the Hartness Bus Company depot. As well as fairs, a market for live pigs and sheep was formerly held in Sandgate. It was also here that bulls were baited prior to slaughter, it being thought this would improve the meat.

PENRITH, *Aerial View c1953* P33019x

The George Hotel, top left, spans the entrance to the Market Arcade in Devonshire Street. It led into a covered market built between 1860 and 1866, a venue much used for meetings and entertainment. On the same side, behind the Musgrave Monument are the white ashlar premises erected for the National Provincial Bank, now housing the National Westminster Bank. Angel Lane is seen on the far right; at the top of the block flanking it once stood the Fleece Inn, and at the lower corner was situated the Angel Inn.

PENRITH
Market Place 1893
32923

A surprisingly tranquil view of the cobbled Market Place on a sunny day in 1893, looking north past the Musgrave Monument into Devonshire Street. The name reminds us that the Duke of Devonshire once owned the rights to the town's markets and fairs. In 1878 the rights were sold to the Penrith Local Board of Health, a forerunner of the local council which now controls them. A traditional Farmers' Market in still held here every third Tuesday in the month, selling local and award-winning specialities, seasonal produce and distinctive crafts.

PENRITH, *Market Place 1893* 32923v

This clock tower monument was erected in 1861 as a memorial to Philip, the eldest son of Sir George and Lady Musgrave of Edenhall, who had died two years earlier in Madrid aged twenty-six. The Musgrave family were one of the most ancient in the area and the monument, a tribute from the town and neighbourhood, was a mark of the high esteem in which they were held. Built of buff-coloured stone in the Victorian Gothic style, it stands in stark contrast with the largely Georgian architecture of the red sandstone buildings that surround it.

PENRITH
Market Place 1893
32923x

Occupying a prime position in the Market Place from 1887 to 1908 was Henry Thompson, Furnishing and General Ironmonger, Black and Whitesmith. In 1909 this property was bought and later demolished by the London City and Midland Bank. They built a new bank on the site, which was completed in 1913.

PENRITH, *Market Place c1955* P33024

This photograph shows the view south across Devonshire Street into King Street. Half hidden by the Musgrave monument is Graham's grocers, established in 1793. By 1991 the adjoining buildings had been demolished to give access to the Angel Lane shopping development. Shops like Boots (extreme far left) relocated there. The baronial revivalist Gothic building on the left afforded smart premises for the Liverpool Bank.

PENRITH, *Market Place 1893* 32923z

Close to the Musgrave Monument is the George Hotel whose substantial premises still occupy most of the buildings on the left hand side of this view. One of the town's oldest inns, it was once known as the George and Dragon. Here Bonnie Prince Charlie rested overnight on his march south during the Jacobite uprising of 1745. Next to the George is the showroom of Thomas Altham and Son, Ironmongers, who occupied these premises until 1914.

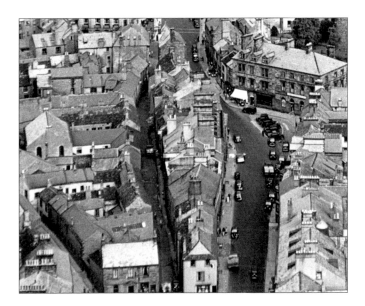

PENRITH
From the Air c1953 P33020v

An island of commercial premises faces right, into King Street, and left, into Rowcliffe Lane. On the left side of King Street is the Robin Hood Inn where in 1794 William Wordsworth cared for his friend and benefactor Raisley Calvert during his terminal illness. On the far left the tall arched windows belong to the Presbyterian Church, now Princes Court apartments.

PENRITH, *King Street c1955* P33022

As we look north towards Market Square, Hutchinson's tobacconist shop is at the corner of Langton Street. Most of the buildings in King Street have remained unchanged except for the Crown Hotel, the bay window of which can be seen on the far right. This old coaching inn opened in 1794 but was demolished some years ago to make way for a modern supermarket.

PENRITH
King Street c1960
P33023

The building here housing the Mitre Hotel in King Street was, in 1826, the birthplace of Penrith's Crimea War hero Trooper William Pearson. Next to it is Armstrong and Fleming's Garage, the offices of the Cumberland & Westmorland Herald, the Horse and Farrier Inn and then Tinkler's Garage.

PENRITH
The Parish Church
1893 32924

In 1716 the parish church of St Andrew was found to be 'in a dangerous and ruinous condition'. It was rebuilt in 1720-22 in the manner of Nicholas Hawksmoor, though the identity of the architect is not known. It incorporates a medieval tower, seen here to the left, which would have been used by the townsfolk as a place of refuge during the days of border warfare.

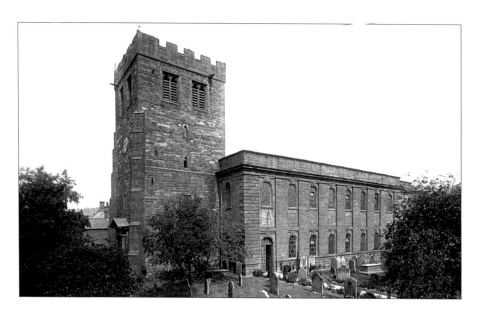

PENRITH, *The Parish Church, the Interior 1893* 32925

St Andrew's has been described as 'the stateliest church of its time in the county'. Inside the nave hang two brass chandeliers which the Duke of Portland presented to the people of Penrith for their loyalty during the Jacobite uprising of 1745. The church also contains mural paintings completed in 1845 by the Penrith-born artist Jacob Thompson. The pews were installed in 1887.

PENRITH, *The Parish Church, the Giant's Grave 1893* 32926

The 'Giant's Grave' in St Andrew's churchyard is a collection of two badly-weathered 10th-century cross-shafts and four Norse 'hogback' tombstones. Stories about the Grave have been linked not only with the mythical giant Sir Owen Caesarius and the Arthurian legends, but also with Owain, son of Urien, a 6th-century king of Rheged, and Owen, King of Cumbria from AD 920 to 937. Beyond is the Gothic-style monument to Robert Virtue, engineer, who supervised the construction of the Lancaster to Carlisle railway which opened in 1846.

PENRITH
Cornmarket c1955
P33013

Waiting patiently before setting off up Castlegate, these cart-horses recall the days when they conveyed farmers, their wives and produce into Cornmarket. Surrounding shops found brisk trade exchanging takings for household wares like drapery, utensils, perquisites and some luxuries like tobacco. Some were of long standing like Joseph Pickering, outfitters, or Edmondson the chemist, who commenced trading there in 1726.

PENRITH, *The Parish Church, the Giant's Thumb 1893* 32927

This monument stands close to the Giant's Grave and is another badly eroded stone cross dating to about the year 920. The carvings on both the Giant's Thumb and Grave show an intriguing mixture of traditional Anglian, Celtic and Norse decorative motifs, indicating that in the 10th century the area around Penrith must have been something of a cultural 'melting pot'. Much later the Giant's Thumb was used as a public pillory.

PENRITH
The Castle 1893 32929

In 1893 Penrith Castle was owned by the London and North Western Railway Company which had stables for their horses inside the ruins. William Strickland is often credited with the building of Penrith Castle. It is more likely, however, to have been constructed for Ralph Neville, Earl of Westmorland and Lord of the Manor of Penrith from 1396 to 1425. The castle was granted to Richard Duke of Gloucester in 1471 and he used it as a base during his period as Lord Warden of the Western Marches. By the mid 1500s it was in a ruinous state and much of the stone was removed for other buildings in the town.

PENRITH, *Middlegate c1955* P33025

From 1670 until 1971 children were taught in Robinson's School, now Penrith Museum, the lowest building on Middlegate's right side. Behind it flows Thacka Beck. Newton's brewery formerly stood adjacent, but by 1911 it had been replaced by the Alhambra entertainment hall, now a cinema. In the 1930s Middlegate experienced a revolution in retailing with the arrival of the chainstores. Burtons and Woolworths altered the streetscape with their respective Art-Deco and stuccoed cost-cutting neo-Georgian designs.

▼ **PENRITH,** *Christ Church 1893* 32929a

Christ Church, which stands between Drover's Lane and Stricklandgate, was consecrated on 31 October 1850. The architects were Travis and Mangnall of Manchester and the builder was Mr Joseph Mawson of Penrith. An increase in the town's population had led to the need for another church and a new burial ground in addition to those of St Andrew's. The burial ground closed in 1873 following the opening of Penrith Cemetery.

▶ **PENRITH**
The Town Hall c1955
P33014

This building was remodelled from two elegant 18th-century Adam-style gentlemen's dwellings. On the left side lived Captain John Wordsworth, the poet Wordsworth's uncle. Its monumentalising face-lift in 1905-6 to provide municipal headquarters and premises for the town's first public library and museum courted controversy. A protest led by Canon Rawnsley, co-founder of the National Trust, succeeded in preserving several original features.

◀ **PENRITH**
*From Elm Terrace
1893* 32922

From the work-yard of George Dixon, builder and mason, we look down on a surviving Penrith institution, Brunswick Road Junior School. The small louvered bell tower overlooks a playground still in use. New substantial dwellings for the town's burgeoning middle class rise up towards Beacon Hill. There, beneath woods owned and managed by the Lowther Estate, the large municipal Penrith Cemetery was opened in 1872 to meet the needs of the expanding town.

▶ **PENRITH**
*Wordsworth Street
1893* 32931A

Like others rising towards Beacon Fell, this terrace, dating from 1865, testifies to the enterprise of the Penrith Building Society. From 1850 it purchased land to develop substantial residences for the town's growing merchant and professional classes. Distinctive red Penrith sandstone was widely used as it had been for the Society's own impressive King Street premises.

PENRITH
Aerial View c1953
P33020

Looking northwards we see hostelries, public houses and stores straddle the streets, highlighting Penrith's importance as a thoroughfare on the London to Carlisle and North East to North West routes. The railway, far left, helped shape its economy stimulating tourism and improving agriculture. The latter benefited from huge quantities of the bird manure 'guano' imported from South America to Whitehaven, carried by rail to the town in tons, and retailed by J and W Maxwell in Cornmarket.

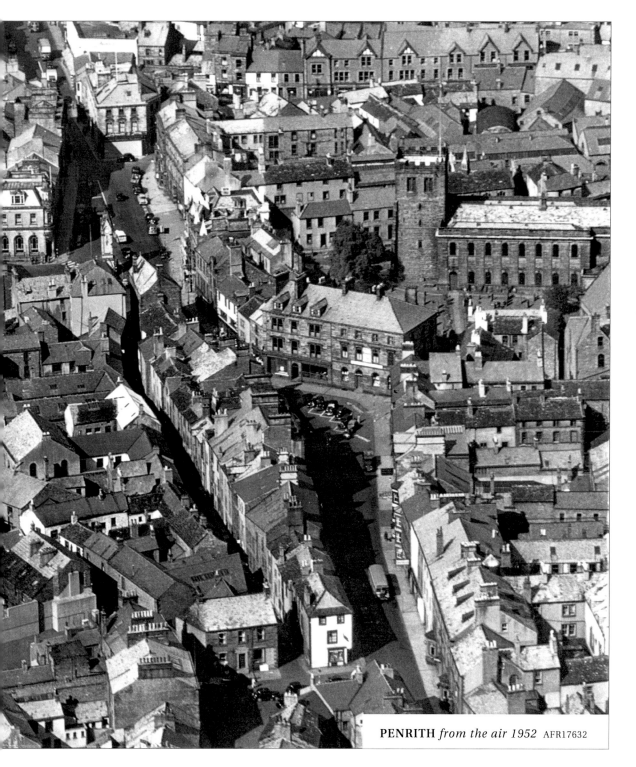

PENRITH *from the air 1952* AFR17632

NORTH TO NUNNERY WALKS

PENRITH, *Edenhall 1893* 32948

Built for Sir George and Lady Musgrave in 1821, Edenhall mansion was designed by Sir Robert Smirke in the Italianate style and replaced an earlier house. The Musgrave family, formerly of Musgrave and later of Harcla Castle in Westmorland, was one of the oldest in the area. They owned the famous 'Luck of Edenhall', a 13th-century Syrian enamelled and gilt glass goblet possibly brought home by a Crusader. It was said to safeguard the family so long as it remained intact and in their ownership. It was sold to the Victoria and Albert Museum before the family estates were broken up. Edenhall was demolished in 1934.

LANGWATHBY
The Bridge c1960
L199017

Before this sandstone bridge was built in 1686, horses and carts crossed the Eden at the 'wath' or ford, which was the longest over the river, hence the name Langwathby. After being swept away by flood-water in the early morning of 25 March 1968 it was replaced by a Bailey bridge, meant to be temporary, but which is still there today.

LANGWATHBY, *The Shepherd's Inn c1955* L199009

In the centre of this spacious village is the War Memorial, standing on the edge of the village green. It was officially 'unveiled' in 1920. The Shepherd's Inn to the right is little changed today, though its car park has been extended to cater for the increase in motor traffic.

FRANCIS FRITH'S - PENRITH

► **LANGWATHBY**
The Green c1960
L199022

The road dividing the
village green in two can
be seen running behind
the bus shelter beside
the tree on the left. The
shelter was erected in
1953 to commemorate
the Coronation of Queen
Elizabeth II. The roundabout
and swings, provided by
the Parochial Foundation
Charity, are still there today.

◀ **LANGWATHBY**
The Post Office c1955
L199001

The bottom green, seen here, was at one time a pond where ducks and geese would wander freely. It was said to have been drained in 1841 by a Mr George Brown. In the centre is Clyde House, once the post office, which along with the village store is now to be found in the converted sandstone barn on the left.

◀ **LANGWATHBY**
The Church c1965
L199029

St Peter's Church, seen here from the churchyard and looking towards the village green, was rebuilt in 1718 on the site of an earlier church. The porch was added in 1836 and in 1883 the roof was heightened and a new east window was inserted.

◄ **LANGWATHBY**
From the Station c1955
L199010

Looking down the hill from above the station, we see the bridge carrying the Settle-Carlisle railway line running along the edge of the village. Opened in 1874 the line was much used for sending timber from Edenhall Woods, as well as local dairy produce and potatoes. The old station now houses a tearoom.

◄ **LAZONBY**
General View c1965
L346035

The land around Lazonby, lying above an impressive curve in the River Eden, presents a tranquil scene here. Once, however, it had been dangerous territory; at nearby Baronwood is the Giant's Chamber, where, according to tradition, people took refuge during Scottish raids. Close by, near Little Salkeld, can be found Long Meg Stone Circle and Lacy's Caves.

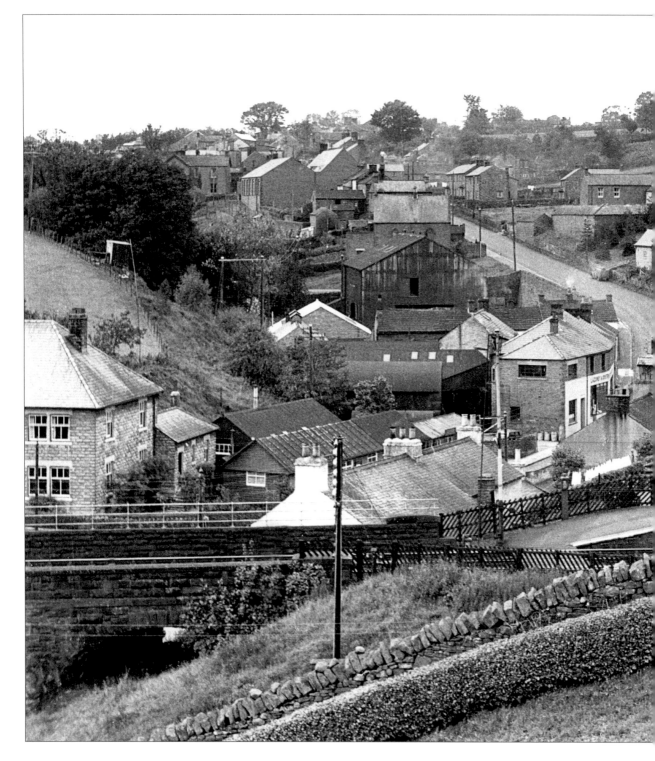

LAZONBY
From the Church Tower L346002

The Settle to Carlisle railway, seen here, brought Lazonby and the surrounding Eden Valley new prosperity, and by 1910 a thriving auction market had been built close to the station from which large amounts of livestock, game and fish were regularly delivered to Yorkshire and London. The former goods shed is still in use, being the centre of production of one of the region's quality bakers.

▲ **LAZONBY,** *The Church c1955* L346306

The church of St Nicholas which dominates this view was
redesigned in 1863 by Anthony Salvin. Not long after, the
enthusiastic wood-carving cleric Canon Wilson adorned the
interior with much of his own work. In the preceding century
its vicar Dr John Brown, a friend of Dr Johnson, had seen his
play 'Barbarossa' produced by David Garrick. Brown's views
on education became famous but his death prevented him
accepting the Empress Catherine's offer to sponsor a visit to
Russia to explain them in greater detail.

◄ **PENRITH,** *The Nunnery Walks Waterfall 1893*
32952

About ten miles north-east of Penrith, near Staffield, pathways have been cut along the banks of the Croglin Beck where it tumbles down through the sandstone gorge it has carved on its way to join the River Eden. The route begins at Nunnery House, a stately mansion built in about 1740 by Henry Aglionby on the site of an ancient Benedictine convent, hence the romantically named 'Nunnery Walks'. Henry's son Christopher is thought to have laid out the walks in about 1770.

PENRITH, *The Nunnery Walks Waterfall 1893* 32950

The scenery around the Nunnery Walks was said to be 'of a most picturesque and sublime description', and the series of cascades and waterfalls here is impressive. The poet William Wordsworth became acquainted with them as a young boy and later, after a visit in 1833, he was inspired to write his sonnet entitled 'Nunnery'.

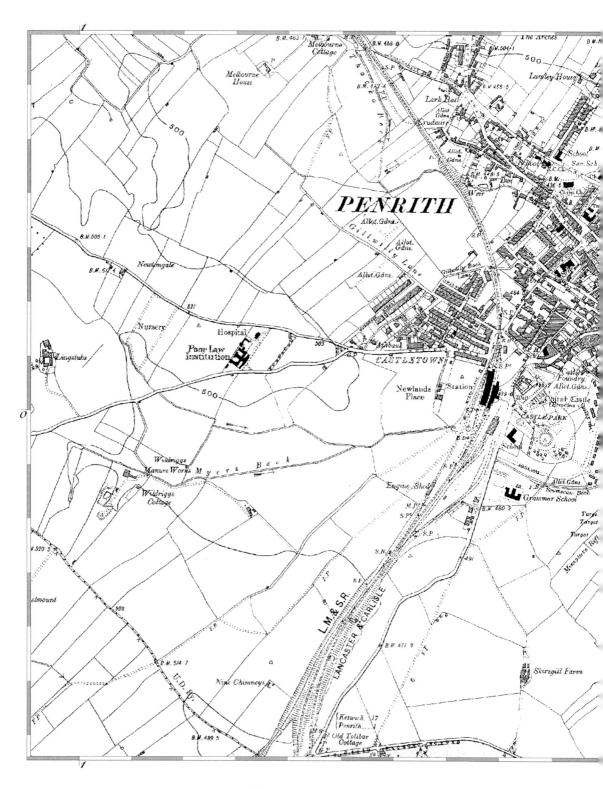

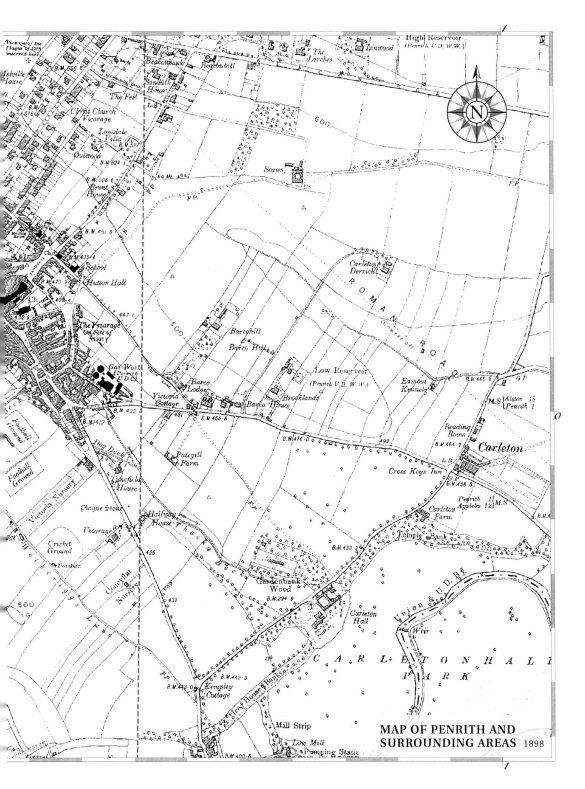

MAP OF PENRITH AND SURROUNDING AREAS 1898

EAST TO MORLAND

EAMONT BRIDGE, *The Bridge 1893* 32934

The old sandstone bridge over the river Eamont, rebuilt in the 16th century, was a popular spot for leisurely strolls from Penrith. The Eamont flows out of Ullswater at Pooley Bridge and is joined by the Lowther at Brougham, before meeting the Eden near Langwathby. Until 1974 the course of the Eamont marked part of the boundary between the old counties of Cumberland and Westmorland.

▲ **EAMONT BRIDGE,** *The Village*
1893 32932

Taylforth's Crown Hotel dates back to 1770 when it was built as a coaching inn. The pony and trap seen here was a versatile form of transport. The coming of the motor car would soon congest the road at its approach to the narrow bridge across the river and traffic lights would eventually control this busy crossing point.

detail of 32932

EAMONT BRIDGE
Mayburgh Henge 1893
32935

Mayburgh Henge is one of a group of three prehistoric monuments near Eamont Bridge. Known collectively as the 'Penrith Henges', the other two are King Arthur's Round Table and the Little Round Table, though little remains of the latter. Early accounts refer to a circle of standing stones inside Mayburgh Henge with four more large stones forming a circle in the centre. Here a visitor gazes quizzically on the only stone now remaining.

PENRITH
*Brougham Castle from
the River Eamont c1873*
6814

Artists and writers have
celebrated the castle ruins
and their setting, notably
J M W Turner and William
Wordsworth. Turner's
evocative and atmospheric
study made in 1809 was used
for his 'Rivers of England'
series of 1825. Wordsworth
recalled pleasant childhood
hours spent exploring them,
linking the building with the
name of Sir Philip Sidney, an
ancestral relative of the castle's
restorer Lady Anne Clifford.

PENRITH
Brougham Castle c1873 6813

Lying alongside the Roman fort 'Brocavum', the castle dates from the 12th century and was held by the Veteripont, and later the Clifford family. In 1420 it was laid waste by the Scots, and damaged in the Civil War. James I was entertained here lavishly in 1617 as the guest of Francis, Earl of Cumberland and his son Henry Clifford. In 1651 the castle was restored by the redoubtable, though charitable, Lady Anne Clifford who died there in 1676.

▼ **PENRITH,** *Brougham Hall from the South West c1873* 6816

Known as the 'Windsor of the North', this mansion in the Gothic style was designed for Lord Henry Brougham (1778-1868), by the architects Cottingham and Hussey. Here in 1894 the Prince of Wales visited Sir Henry Charles Brougham and his wife Zoë. Following the sale of the mansion in 1934 parts of it were demolished, then during the Second World War it hosted, with Lowther Castle, a secret CDL Tank project. Partly restored, Brougham Hall now houses a variety of creative initiatives.

▼ **TEMPLE SOWERBY,** *The Village c1955* T289005

Temple Sowerby commemorates the Knights Templar who afforded protection to pilgrims journeying to Jerusalem and held the manor here for over a century and a half. Following the suppression of the Knights Templar, in 1323 the Knights Hospitallers succeeded them, holding the manor for over two centuries until 1543 following the dissolution of religious houses. The present manor house, Acorn Bank, dates from 1656. An historic herb garden, open to the public, is cared for here by the National Trust.

▶ **TEMPLE SOWERBY**
The King's Arms Hotel
c1955 T289002

Set back from the A66, the King's Arms with its stables and courtyard to the rear was once a coaching-house serving travellers on the Penrith to Darlington turnpike, a route linking the Lakes, the Eden Valley and Stainmore with Durham and Yorkshire. Next to it stands the Church of St James, built in 1754, enlarged sixteen years later, then following a century of use restored in 1873.

EAST TO MORLAND

◀ **MORLAND**
General View
c1955 M98008

Well-nourished lambs,
unshorn fleeces
and lush foliage
tell us that summer
has just begun in
this pastoral idyll.
Livestock including
sheep, cattle, poultry
as well as agricultural
produce were the
mainstay of the
villages surrounding
Penrith until relatively
recent times. They
supplied the town's
numerous markets
until the railways
opened up more
distant ones.

▶ **MORLAND**
The Village 1893
32964

'Morlund', an ancient
spelling preserving the
word 'lundr', suggests
that hereabouts Norse
settlers entertained
a superstitious awe
for a wood or sacred
grove set upon or
close by moorland or
marsh. A sylvan charm
is certainly evident
in this scene, one
enhanced by the beck
which flows through
the village before
joining the River
Lyvennet.

▶ **MORLAND**
Lowergate c1955 M98003

Morland, remarkably, was
not spared the march of
industry characteristic of
the Victorian age. Here,
by the early 19th century,
two factories were making
coarse linen goods and
specialising in tapes,
threads and small wares.
The Carlisle Savings Bank
opened a branch at Morland
in 1839 in the wake of their
prosperity. Literacy in turn
seems to have improved at
that time for by 1849 the
village had its own library.

◀ **MORLAND**
Riverside c1955 M98010

Though cars were more affordable by the 1950s, engines, being thirstier by today's standards, needed more frequent refueling. Kirkpatrick's, like many a village garage, provided services once the domain of the wayside blacksmith – keeping conveyances in running order. Filling up was once a leisurely, almost social business performed by the proprietor; here once the car was catered for you could even top up next door with tea.

MORLAND
The Church 1893 32966

The church of St Lawrence originally belonged to the Abbey of St Mary at York and income from it was used to support the Priory at Wetheral. Though picturesque, the ivy engulfing the church in this view obscures a feature rare in the region – a pre-Conquest western tower. One of its bells, dated 1687, was made by Lancelot Smith of Penrith. The church underwent a major restoration within two years of this photograph.

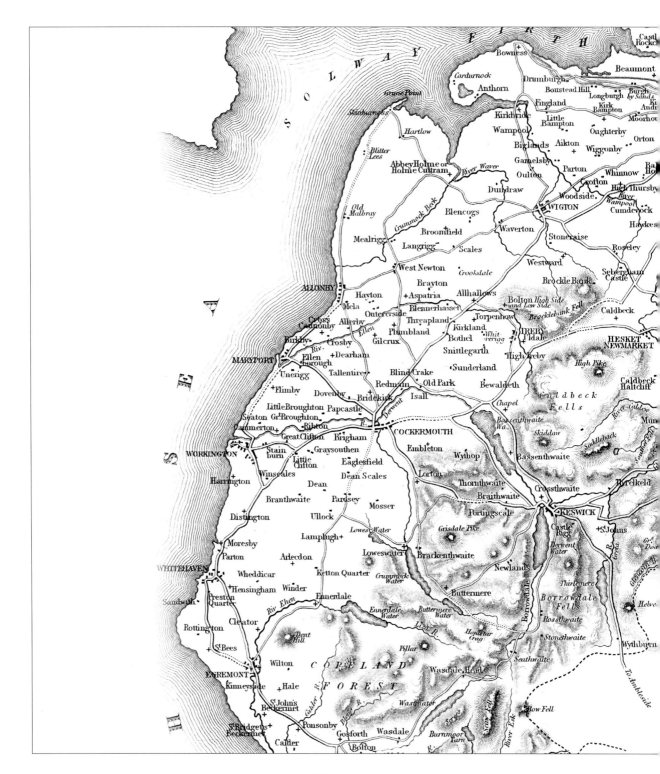

SOUTH TO HAWESWATER

TIRRIL *c1955* T359006

The motor-car opened up the Lakes to many families previously constrained by limited leisure time and travel distance. The 'day trip' was born. It brought new trade to outlying village hostelries such as this one at Tirril. The Queen's Head once belonged to the Wordsworth family whose roots lay in neighbouring Sockbridge and Penrith.

TIRRIL, *From the Penrith Road c1955*
T359007

From Tirril, midway between Penrith and Ullswater, a road leads to Sockbridge. This was the home of Wordsworth's grandfather Richard, and his father John. Both had been employed by the local magnates, the Lowther family, to manage their lands. This corner of Cumbria abounds in associations with the poet. His recollection of a walk in brisk weather over nearby Barton Fell for instance lies behind some of the imagery of his poem 'The Leech Gatherer'.

TIRRIL, *The Institute c1955* T359002

The Institute and Reading Room, built in an eclectic Arts and Crafts style, recalls the contribution to that Movement made by local protagonists like John Ruskin, Albert Fleming, W G Collingwood and Canon Hardwicke Rawnsley. The latter two had acknowledged the influence on the Movement of Quaker simplicity in life-style and design. Many influential followers of that faith had lived around Tirril, including Sir Thomas Clarkson and Thomas Wilkinson. For many years Slee's Quaker Mathematical Academy flourished in Tirril.

PENRITH, *Askham Bridge 1893* 32945

Forming a picturesque scene near Askham, the bridge arches over the River Lowther whose waters have their origin in the north-east Lakeland fells above Shap. Further down, the river forms a pond and falls over a weir flowing to join the River Eamont. The combined waters then enter the River Eden. The surrounding countryside inspired artists like Peter de Wint and the local prodigy Jacob Thompson. As a youth the latter was discovered by Lord Lowther sketching its beauties, a chance encounter which won him the support of the Earl who cultivated links with men of arts and letters.

TIRRIL, *Tongue Gill c1930* T359001

Here the Ullswater and Helvellyn fells present a magnificent view but changeable weather and difficult terrain can turn it into a formidable one. Its victims include Charles Gough who fell to his death on Helvellyn's Striding Edge where months later his dog was found alive, still guarding his remains. Gough, a Quaker, was buried in Tirril in the graveyard adjoining the Meeting House. He and his dog were immortalised in the poems 'Helvellyn' by Sir Walter Scott, and 'Fidelity' by William Wordsworth.

PENRITH
Lowther Castle 1894
33514

Built to replace the ruinous Lowther Hall, damaged by fire in 1720, the Castle was designed by Sir Robert Smirke for William Lowther, Earl of Lonsdale. Construction began in 1806 and took five years to complete. The north front, seen here, exceeds 400ft in length. It survived intact until the 1950s when its contents and fittings were auctioned. Though largely dismantled, the shell of the façade and tower were fortunately preserved. In 1895 Kaiser Wilhelm II stayed here as the guest of Lord Lowther.

PENRITH
Lowther Lodge 1893
32937

This castellated building dating from 1877 was designed for Henry Lowther, 3rd Earl of Lonsdale to guard the entrance to the drive up to Lowther Castle. It is in keeping with the neo-Gothic architecture of the latter. Above the door can be seen their shield of six annulets which, in heraldry are painted black on a shield of gold. The latter colour, being dominant, rendered their livery quite dramatic. The succeeding Earl, the keen sportsman Hugh Lowther, used it to great effect on his fleet of motor-cars gaining him the nick-name 'The Yellow Earl'.

▶ **PENRITH**
Hugh's Crag Bridge
1893 32943

On 18 July 1844 the London and North Western Railway Company began work to extend the railway from Lancaster to Carlisle. By 15 December 1846, and at a cost of £22,000 per mile, this remarkable feat of engineering had been completed. It had negotiated a tidal river, deep valleys and cut through great banks of rock rising over 900ft to cross Shap Fell. Here the viaduct carries it at a height of 100ft.

◄ **SHAP**
*The Shap Wells Hotel
1893* 32971

The hotel, which opened in 1833, was built to serve the growing numbers of visitors to the natural spring in its grounds, whose waters were believed to be 'very efficacious in several diseases'. Under the ownership of the Earl of Lonsdale it became a fashionable resort, and was visited by Princess Mary in the 1920s and 30s. During the Second World War the hotel was requisitioned as a prisoner of war camp for German officers.

HAWESWATER *1893*
32980

In 1893 the natural lake
of Haweswater nestled
peacefully in the unspoilt
and beautiful valley of
Mardale. At this time the
road to Mardale village ran
along the west side of the
lake. Not many years later,
following the Haweswater
Act of 1919, Manchester
Corporation would be given
the right to acquire the
lake and its surrounding
catchment area for a major
reservoir. The completion
of the scheme took a while,
but by the late 1930s the
demolished remains of the
village lay drowned under
the waters of the flooded
valley.

MARDALE
The Church 1893 32977

Holy Trinity Church was built in the late 17th century, probably on the site of a medieval oratory founded by monks from Shap Abbey. The six ancient yews which surrounded it were said to be even older and grew higher than the tower. The first burial in the churchyard was in 1729; until then coffins were strapped to pack horses and taken by the 'corpse road' over Mardale Common for burial at Shap. In 1936 the church was demolished and about one hundred coffins were exhumed for reburial at Shap cemetery.

MARDALE, *Castle Crag 1893* 32976

On the summit of Castle Crag, in the centre of the photograph, are the remains of an early British fort. All the buildings in this view, including the farm at Flake How seen here to the left, were demolished before the flooding of the valley. Gone too is Measand Beck Hall which was close by. Here the Penrith-born artist Jacob Thompson had often stayed with the Blands while on his painting trips to the area.

HAWESWATER, *The Dam c1960* H541016

Work on the dam started in 1930 using stone quarried locally, but its construction was
delayed for a while and restarted in 1934. The dam is of the 'hollow massive-buttress'
type. It is 96ft high and 1550ft long. The surface area of Haweswater Reservoir, when
full, is three times greater than that of the natural lake it replaced.

77

WEST TO GREYSTOKE AND ULLSWATER

GREYSTOKE, *The Castle 1893* 32955

Described as an 'ambitious and correct neo-Elizabethan mansion', Greystoke Castle was remodelled by Anthony Salvin in 1839-48 and again after a fire of 1868. Its romantic façade replaced an earlier structure built for Henry Charles Howard around 1675. Salvin incorporated a medieval pele tower which William, 14th Baron of Greystoke, had been given permission to fortify in 1353.

GREYSTOKE, *The Church 1893*
32959

Dedicated to St Andrew, this church is surprisingly large because William de Greystoke obtained a royal licence in 1358 to establish a college here to replace a simple cruciform church. However, it was not until 1382 that the college was finally founded by Ralph, Lord Greystoke. The priests of the college were 'chantry priests' who offered masses for the souls of the dead, their founder and benefactors. The college was closed at the time of the Reformation when chantries were abolished and St Andrew's returned to being a rectory. The church underwent major restoration in the 19th century, though some medieval features remain.

GREYSTOKE, *The Green c1965* G266030

The centre of the village, with its attractive houses round the green, is marked by a market cross reminding us that Henry III had granted a license to Thomas de Greystoke for a weekly market and fair. Behind the cross can be glimpsed the Boot and Shoe Inn, an old coaching inn dating from the 17th century.

GREYSTOKE
The Village c1955 G266013

The growth of the urban one-stop convenience store and filling station unexpectedly reflects a return to the situation found here, where F & F Hawell's shop is located next to the village petrol pump. Improved communications are indicated by the telegraph poles but the absence of roof-top aerials shows that the television had yet to find a place in every home.

► **PENRITH**
Hutton John 1893 32953

Hutton John was anciently part of the Baronry of Greystoke, and was held by the Hutton family. When Thomas Hutton died without an heir in the reign of Elizabeth I, the estate passed by marriage to Andrew Huddleston and the mansion became the main residence of the Huddleston family. It began as a square castellated pele tower to which was added a hall range. It was further extended and modernised in the 19th century.

◀ **PENRITH**
Blencow Hall 1893 32961

This hall near Greystoke was built with defence in mind. The pele towers of such buildings protected owners, their livestock and goods against raiding Scots and from the lawlessness to which they were more vulnerable due to the remoteness of the region. The Act of Union ended border warfare and Henry Blencow who lived here was knighted by King James I and became Sheriff of Cumberland

PENRITH, *Ennim 1893* 32954

About half a mile south of the village of Blencow is the house
known as Ennim Bank. The name derives from 'innam', meaning
a piece of land which was enclosed or taken in. It is thought to
have been the original residence of the Blencow family before
they moved to Blencow Hall. In the mid 19th century George
Troutbeck greatly improved the mansion and ornamented it with
'plantations'. More recently it was the home of Viscount William
Whitelaw of Penrith until his death in 1999.

PENRUDDOCK, *The Village c1955* P334012

Penruddock is a small village on the edge of the Lake District
National Park, about five miles west of Penrith. Its name is
thought to be Celtic in origin. The slightly raised location affords
fine views of the Lake District hills to the west and south. The
view is of the east end of the village, looking towards Saddleback.
Modern buildings have since replaced some shown here.

ULLSWATER
The View at Aira Force 20571

This was an attraction as early as 1799 when Wordsworth and Coleridge visited it. A tale is attached to this scenic waterfall: a lady, long separated from her suitor knight, was found by him sleepwalking along its banks. His touch awoke her but being startled she fell into its waters and tragically drowned.

ULLSWATER, *Purse Point c1955* U4001

Here a group of visitors pause to admire the view from Purse Point across the lake towards Glenridding. Ullswater, or 'Ulph's-water', takes its name from the Viking settler Lyulph, whose name was popularised in the 18th century when the Duke of Norfolk, then owner of Greystoke Castle, built the folly called Lyulph's Tower on the north side of the lake.

INDEX

AROUND PENRITH

Aerial View 16, 17, 23, 34-35,
            36-37
Askham Bridge 66-67
The Beacon 15, 16
Blencow Hall 82-83
Brougham Castle 54-55
Christ Church 32
Cornmarket 28-29
Edenhall 38
Elm Terrace 32-33
Ennim 84
Hugh's Crag Bridge 72-73
Hutton John 82-83
King Street 23, 24-25
Lowther Castle 68-69
Lowther Lodge 70-71
Market Place 18-19, 20, 21
Middlegate 31
The Nunnery Walks 47
The Parish Church 26, 27, 30
Penrith Castle 31
The Town Hall 32
Wordsworth Street 33

LANGWATHBY

The Bridge 39
The Church 42
From The Station 42-43
The Green 40-41
The Post Office 40-41
The Shepherd's Inn 39

LAZONBY

From The Church 44-45, 46
General View 43

EAMONT BRIDGE

The Bridge 50
Mayburgh Henge 52-53
The Village 51

TEMPLE SOWERBY

The King's Arm Hotel 56
The Village 56

MORLAND

The Church 60-61
General View 56-57
Lowergate 58-59
Riverside 58-59
The Village 57

HAWESWATER

The Dam 77
General View 74-75

MARDALE

Castle Crag 76
The Church 76

THE SHAP WELLS HOTEL

72-73

TIRRIL

From The Penrith Road 65
General View 64
The Institute 65
Tongue Gill 66-67

GREYSTOKE

The Castle 78
The Church 79
The Green 79
The Village 80-81

PENRUDDOCK

The Village 85

ULLSWATER

Purse Point 86
The View at Aira Force 86

NAMES OF PRE-PUBLICATION BUYERS

THE FOLLOWING PEOPLE HAVE KINDLY SUPPORTED THIS BOOK BY
SUBSCRIBING TO COPIES BEFORE PUBLICATION.

D G Adams, The Station, Long Marton, Westmorland

To Ann from Dad & Mam, Blencowe

Sheila Rose Armstrong

The Ashton-Ridley Family

Howard, Heather, Daniel & Charlotte Bateman

Stephen & Sandra Batty, Penrith

The Beaty Family, Sockbridge

Michelle Bell

To Gordon Bennison on Fathers Day 2005

To Susan & Mark Blackshaw from Ann & Anthony

The Booker Family, Newton Reigny, Penrith

The Booth Family of Kings Meaburn

To Len Borrowdale with love

Mr & Mrs J S Boulton, Carlisle

Geoffrey Bowerbank, Penrith

The Bracken Family, Penrith

Gordon Browne, Penrith

Mariline & Robert Burns, Appleby

John & Moyra Burrell

Richard Hugh Burton

A N & S A Carr, Penrith

N Carr & C A Carr, Ponteland

Jennifer Carrick, Penrith

In memory of Mr J & M Clement, Penrith

Melville Clementson

Miss M V Collins, Penrith

For Geoff & Elsie Creighton, Penrith

Pete Davies, Coventry - Penrith by choice

John, Liz, Debbie & Jono Davis, Penrith

To Kevin & Annette Dixon, Penrith

Keith George Dudson

Stephen Dudson

The Dunn Family, Low Woodside, Brougham

Bob, Dorothy & Les Eastham, Askham

To Keith Elliott, Penrith, with love

Robert & Joy Emerson, Brougham, Penrith

Mr & Mrs R D Emmerson & Family, Penrith

Robert Michael Eyres, Shap, 2005

Tyrone & Mandy Fletcher, Tollbar, Edenhall

The Furness Family, Penrith

Peter Gates

In memory of the Gilpin Family of Penrith

To Ron & Betty Glaister on your Golden Wedding, love Shirley & John

Ian Glendinning, Penrith

Raymond Glendinning, Penruddock

To Grandma, Happy Birthday, love Shona

The Grant Family, Mary Taphouse

Jim Greenop 1937-05, dear Husband of Gill

To Martin Hall, thanks from The Emersons

Tony Harrison

To John Rodney Heath on his birthday

The Hindson Family, Penrith

Bill & Annie Hodgson

E Hodgson, Kirkby Thore and C & P Window, London

The Humphreys Family, Penrith

To Norman & June Hunter

Mr A E & Mrs I H Hunter, Penrith

W E Ivinson

L G & K S M Jarman

In memory of W Johnston, Penrith

Tracey Jones, Blencarn

In memory of Mrs Louisa Jordan, Duke St, Penrith

Ron J Kirby, Skelton, Penrith

Ellen Patricia Knight

Linda & David, Hutton End

Dr Bryan C Lindley, Dr Judith A Heyworth

In memory of Richard & Hannah Little

To Brian Lumby on your 50th Birthday, love Mam
Loving memories of my Dad Jack Lumby, love Ann
John T Lund, ex-inspector Cumbria Police
Alan McViety
Raymond Bernard Macro, Penrith 1941
The Mandales, Brunswick Square, Penrith
Margaret & Peter Manning, Harrogate
In memory of F C Martin, Penrith
T W Moore, Penrith
K L Murphy who loves old photographs
Maria Murray
Chelsea & Norris Nicholson
To Mum Vera Nixon, Happy Birthday 01/05/05
Mary Pallister, Green Acres, Blencowe
Joseph Parker, Kirkoswald
Robert Parker, Kirkoswald
Especially for you Daddy, love Zak Parkin
Grandad Parkin, Morland, love little Jimmy
Dorrie & Michael Phillips
The Pickering family, Penrith
In memory of Harry Piggott
Les & Jean Pluckrose, Diamond Anniversary
Malc & Liz Pochec - True Friends, from Pete
P F Power, Warsop, Nottinghamshire
William James Reed, Plumpton, Penrith
The Ridley Family
The Ridley Family, Penrith
Rosalind & David Robinson
J M Robinson, Penrith
For Rita & Stan Rooke, Appleby, Cumbria
Irene Rumney, Penrith
Major John Henry Crackanthorpe Sawrey-Cookson
The Sayer Family
In memory of Fred & Jane Seagrave, Penrith

Richard & Kathleen Sealby
H & J Shuttleworth, USA (Penrith)
T W Skelton and Family, Newby, Penrith
Sheila A Smith
The Stanaway Family, Askham
Michael Steadman, Newton
Eden & Morgan Stephenson, Penrith
Willie & Theresa Stephenson
To Mrs D M Strong, Sleagill
The Strong Family, Sleagill
The Swainson Family, Penrith
The Taylor Family, Bolton
Hazel Teasdale, 'Don't forget us'
Hugh T & Valerie A Thompson
Clara Thwaites, married 1853, Watermillock
Mr G S & Mrs S A Tothill, Scarrows, Lazonby
Frank & Hazel Tyson, Blencowe
Harvey & Gwen Veitch, Langwathby
The Ware Family, Penrith
Marlene & Ed Ware and Family
Patricia Watson, 'Happy Birthday'
The Family of C J & B E Wilson, Penrith
The Woof Family, Penrith
Kevin & Denise Wynne, Langwathby

FRITH PRODUCTS & SERVICES

Francis Frith would doubtless be pleased to know that the pioneering publishing venture he started in 1860 still continues today. Over a hundred and forty years later, The Francis Frith Collection continues in the same innovative tradition and is now one of the foremost publishers of vintage photographs in the world. Some of the current activities include:

Interior Decoration

Today Frith's photographs can be seen framed and as giant wall murals in thousands of pubs, restaurants, hotels, banks, retail stores and other public buildings throughout the country. In every case they enhance the unique local atmosphere of the places they depict and provide reminders of gentler days in an increasingly busy and frenetic world.

Product Promotions

Frith products are used by many major companies to promote the sales of their own products or to reinforce their own history and heritage. Frith promotions have been used by Hovis bread, Courage beers, Scots Porage Oats, Colman's mustard, Cadbury's foods, Mellow Birds coffee, Dunhill pipe tobacco, Guinness, and Bulmer's Cider.

Genealogy and Family History

As the interest in family history and roots grows world-wide, more and more people are turning to Frith's photographs of Great Britain for images of the towns, villages and streets where their ancestors lived; and, of course, photographs of the churches and chapels where their ancestors were christened, married and buried are an essential part of every genealogy tree and family album.

Frith Products

All Frith photographs are available Framed or just as Mounted Prints and Posters (size 23 x 16 inches). These may be ordered from the address below. From time to time other products - Address Books, Calendars, Table Mats, etc - are available.

The Internet

Already ninety thousand Frith photographs can be viewed and purchased on the internet through the Frith websites and a myriad of partner sites.

For more detailed information on Frith companies and products, look at these sites:

www.francisfrith.co.uk
www.francisfrith.com
(for North American visitors)

See the complete list of Frith Books at:

www.francisfrith.co.uk

This web site is regularly updated with the latest list of publications from The Francis Frith Collection. If you wish to buy books relating to another part of the country that your local bookshop does not stock, you may purchase on-line.

For further information, trade, or author enquiries please contact us at the address below:
The Francis Frith Collection, Frith's Barn, Teffont, Salisbury, Wiltshire, England SP3 5QP.
Tel: +44 (0)1722 716 376 Fax: +44 (0)1722 716 881 Email: sales@francisfrith.co.uk

---

See Frith books on the internet at www.francisfrith.co.uk

FREE PRINT OF YOUR CHOICE

Mounted Print
Overall size 14 x 11 inches (355 x 280mm)

Choose any Frith photograph in this book.
Simply complete the Voucher opposite and
return it with your remittance for £3.50 (to cover
postage and handling) and we will print the
photograph of your choice in SEPIA (size 11 x 8
inches) and supply it in a cream mount with a
burgundy rule line (overall size 14 x 11 inches).
**Please note: aerial photographs and
photographs with a reference number
starting with a "Z" are not Frith photographs
and cannot be supplied under this offer.
Offer valid for delivery to one UK address only.**

PLUS: **Order additional Mounted Prints
at HALF PRICE - £9.50 each** (normally £19.00)
If you would like to order more Frith prints from
this book, possibly as gifts for friends and family,
you can buy them at half price (with no
additional postage and handling costs).

PLUS: **Have your Mounted Prints framed**
For an extra £18.00 per print you can have your
mounted print(s) framed in an elegant polished
wood and gilt moulding, overall size
16 x 13 inches (no additional postage and
handling required).

IMPORTANT!

These special prices are only available if you use
this form to order. You must use the ORIGINAL
VOUCHER on this page (no copies permitted). We
can only despatch to one UK address. This offer
cannot be combined with any other offer.

Send completed Voucher form to:
**The Francis Frith Collection, Frith's Barn,
Teffont, Salisbury, Wiltshire SP3 5QP**

CHOOSE A PHOTOGRAPH FROM THIS BOOK

Voucher for **FREE**
and Reduced Price
Frith Prints

*Please do not photocopy this voucher. Only the original is valid,
so please fill it in, cut it out and return it to us with your order.*

Picture ref no	Page no	Qty	Mounted @ £9.50	Framed + £18.00	Total Cost £
		1	Free of charge*	£	£
			£9.50	£	£
			£9.50	£	£
			£9.50	£	£
			£9.50	£	£
			£9.50	£	£

*Please allow 28 days
for delivery.
Offer available to one
UK address only*

* Post & handling		£3.50
Total Order Cost		**£**

Title of this book . . . .

I enclose a cheque/postal order for £ . . . .
made payable to 'The Francis Frith Collection'

OR please debit my Mastercard / Visa / Maestro card,
details below

Card Number

Issue No (Maestro only)   Valid from (Maestro)

Expires   Signature

Name Mr/Mrs/Ms . . . .
Address . . . .
. . . .
. . . .
. . . . Postcode . . . .
Daytime Tel No . . . .
Email . . . .

Valid to 31/12/12

Would you like to find out more about Francis Frith?

We have recently recruited some entertaining speakers who are happy to visit local groups, clubs and societies to give an illustrated talk documenting Frith's travels and photographs. If you are a member of such a group and are interested in hosting a presentation, we would love to hear from you.

Our speakers bring with them a small selection of our local town and county books, together with sample prints. They are happy to take orders. A small proportion of the order value is donated to the group who have hosted the presentation. The talks are therefore an excellent way of fundraising for small groups and societies.

Can you help us with information about any of the Frith photographs in this book?

We are gradually compiling an historical record for each of the photographs in the Frith archive. It is always fascinating to find out the names of the people shown in the pictures, as well as insights into the shops, buildings and other features depicted.

If you recognize anyone in the photographs in this book, or if you have information not already included in the author's caption, do let us know. We would love to hear from you, and will try to publish it in future books or articles.

Our production team

Frith books are produced by a small dedicated team at offices in the converted Grade II listed 18th-century barn at Teffont near Salisbury, illustrated above. Most have worked with the Frith Collection for many years. All have in common one quality: they have a passion for the Frith Collection. The team is constantly expanding, but currently includes:

Paul Baron, Jason Buck, John Buck, Ruth Butler, Heather Crisp, David Davies, Louis du Mont, Isobel Hall, Lucy Hart, Julian Hight, Peter Horne, James Kinnear, Karen Kinnear, Tina Leary, Stuart Login, Sue Molloy, Glenda Morgan, Wayne Morgan, Sarah Roberts, Kate Rotondetto, Dean Scource, Eliza Sackett, Terence Sackett, Sandra Sampson, Adrian Sanders, Sandra Sanger, Julia Skinner, David Turner, Miles Smith, Lewis Taylor, Shelley Tolcher, Lorraine Tuck, Miranda Tunniclisse, Amanita Wainwright and Ricky Williams.